Journey of a Father

Lessons Learned from Terah

ISBN: 978-1-942421-23-8

By: Rodney A Drury

RMM

1919 Sunnyview Drive

Peoria IL 61614

Table of Contents

Table of Contents

Markers

Just north of Butte, Nebraska there is an old cottonwood tree that overshadows a graveyard. In summer, when the tree is full of leaves the shadow just touches two burial plots.

The markers have names and dates, but you can't read them. Winter, mold, pollen, dirt have all joined together to help hide the couple. On the right is an old dirt farmer. To the left, his wife. Both have impacted the world. Both are not hidden.

The tractor path to the graveyard hasn't been used for years. People are not buried here anymore. It's not that the three-hundred and fifty residents of Butte don't want to be buried here, they are just too practical to pay the prices required to get people from "town" to come out and open a grave site. It's more sensible just be cremated and ship the remains back to the family, wherever they are.

I wouldn't know about this couple except that they are my grandparents. It is through them I exist: one tall and lanky dirt farmer who created in me a respect for the Midwest's idea of redneck. And his praying wife who imparted to me a mystical spirit.

At times I fall into the delusion that I am a product of my own endeavors. I am not. My family gave life to me. And that life includes a living history of hard work, intercession, love for the outdoors and from time to time, a sneaking out behind the barn for some self-indulgence.

Most world history is not full of digital media and records. If we look back to those who lived just a hundred years ago, we will find gravestones or physical records of census, immigration, birth records or family Bibles. If we compare the past to today we realize just how easy it is today for everyone to have a historical record.

"Terah" is a name you will stumble across when reading about the family line of Jesus and Abraham. His story takes up less than a few of hundred words in the Bible. And he is the father of the man who becomes known as the Father of the Faith.

Come join me as we investigate this life that is hidden off the pathway. Join me in departing from the common and searching out a life that God used to build a nation.

What can we learn from Terah that will help us father today? What does this hidden man reveal to us about the ways of God and the flow of life?

Terah

Terah was off the beaten pathway. If we read right past the comments about him, we will not see how Terah can help us understand pain and suffering. We will miss the man who grandfathered the faith.

Like all of us, Terah appears in history at just the right time. If he was alive today he would be a man who would encapsule the famous verse, "for such a time as this." (Esther 4:4) Here's why.

The downward spiral of humanity seems to hit rock bottom in Genesis 11. A global event of rebellion where humanity seeks to reach God by their own effort is defeated by God. The result is a world of broken communication. People are unable to understand one another. They are scattered over the face of the earth.

Then the stories in the Bible turn into a list of names. As though a part of history was too boring to describe, or maybe to hopeless to disclose, we get a record of who lived, how long and a list of their male children. Decades of history fly by with the reading of each name.

Each name is a link in history. Each person, those mentioned and those not, are a part of God's plan for divine reversal. It will take thousands of years to unfold. But even the plans of God need to begin somewhere.

When life seems to be at its lowest, God enacts His plan of redemption. It is a plan that is not hurried. It is a plan that involves humanity. It is a plan that involves both the fathers and sons, the old and the young. It is a union of fathers: a cooperation of a dad in heaven and men on earth. It reveals our heritage.

Each one of us comes from two places. We come from our biological families, and we come from our spiritual forefathers. You did not arrive here on your own. Others have gone before. Some may have been a part of a rebellion against God. Others might seem to be little more than a name on a page of history, a link in your family line, but little else. And others seem to be a hinge that opens a door to a new day, a new time, a new season of God's grace.

While we all would choose to be significant, perhaps what we really mean is that we would all like to be someone special. And in that desire, we make judgments and decisions that affect our identity and worth.

Terah is not a superhero. Terah is not a big deal in most of our Bible books or study notes. The most common comment I have heard about Terah over the years is that he represents a man who made it only halfway. Terah is often portrayed as a failed follower who needed his son to finish the job.

That popular belief might not be right. What is most commonly seen is seldom at the heart of a matter and never at the heart of a man. Hidden treasures, riches, motives, and desires are buried in each of us. Our everyday life seldom depicts our dreams. We need wisdom and caution when it comes to judging.

How do we judge rightly the worth of a man's life? Is it only by what they have accomplished?

Do some men do little more than keep the line going and in so doing fulfill all that God asks of them?

Are all men, all fathers, mostly failures unless something notable is accomplished through them?

Do I have a prejudice that affects my value judgments? Do I see accomplishment connected to worth?

If I took time with the Lord and inquired into the worth of a man's life, what might the Lord say to my heart?

If you first discovered Terah in the New Testament, you found him in a list of names from Adam to Jesus. A list that speaks to humanity of our common origin.

We Are One People

The Bible and our world both reveal to us that we are surrounded by different kinds of people, nations, and tribes. But the Bible also clearly teaches us that we are all one people.

The Jewish nation is about to be birthed through Terah's son. Jews came from Gentiles. And that revelation should open our understanding and emotions toward all races.

Regardless of how divided we are now, regardless of how much you cling to your racial identity or cultural history, if you go back far enough you will discover we are all one people.

Our unity as one people does not negate the reality of many tongues, tribes, nations, and people. Diversity is here. We are not all the same.

It was a Father in heaven who started this race.

It was fathers on earth who kept it going and growing.

Fathers play a role in redemption. They play a role in division too. Fathers can be men who hate diversity or fear it. Fathers can be people who launch new degrees of diversity and know how to unite people in the name of the Lord.

As a father you have an obligation to your family line. You also have an obligation to your Heavenly Father's family line. All our personal identities are related to Him. All our unique family history is a part of His history.

Understanding three things will help you help your family.

1. Covenant Relationships
2. Promise
3. Redemption

Covenant relationships are clear statements from God about His purpose and intentions. They are an agreement that He will perform what He promised.

Promise, especially in the New Testament, is the specific content God communicates to a person.

Redemption is the plan of God to redeem each person on the earth. It is the ongoing story of our Father in heaven seeking sons and daughters to be forever united as family.

Your story is a part of that story.

Your calling, identity, and purpose are all a part of God's redemption, promises and covenant relationships.

How can you live fearlessly and with an open heart to all the diversity on the earth and still fulfill your role as a father to a specific group?

How well do you understand that like Terah you are not called to do everything, but instead have a limited task, a specific focus, and a limited time on earth?

Do you have a clear understanding of God's covenant relationship with you? Do you know what God has promised to do for you?

Or do you mainly pick promises and examples from the Bible and try to make them your own? It is true that the nature of God is steadfast, but His callings and purposes for each of our lives varies greatly. You do not need to choose your promises. Instead live open and free with the Holy Spirit and God's Spirit will lead you into a full and whole redeeming relationship with Him, including clear specific promises.

Self-Governance

When we read the story that is in the Bible, we can clearly see that God is showing us His story. But when we live His history, it mostly feels like we are swimming around in our own ocean. The connections to God are often unfelt or not noticed.

We may think that the world is governed by personal choice. We can think that destiny is a matter of personal empowerment. That life takes a person somewhere depending on their vision, their focus, or their passions.

While passion, focus, and vision are a part of life, they do not rule.

Yes, I know that does not appear to be true. I know that in some countries it appears like you can be and do whatever you want if you believe enough or are driven enough.

But that is where fathers come in.

Like our Father in heaven, earthly fathers may teach us to live with passion and remain under the rule of the Lord. Both God and dads can give us vision. Both can help us when we need to focus.

Fathers can teach us how to live a unified and happy life, not for self, but for God. Fathers help children learn to live free while at the same time staying connected in family, understanding boundaries, and enjoying limits.

The great fall in the garden of Eden was a result of *personal* vision and governance. Choosing to self-govern, early humanity chose self-rule. And we, like them, tend to do the same thing.

Terah is an example to us. We see that life was going on and on for Terah's family line. Then God invaded their rule. God spoke to a father. Terah did not cause the birth of a new nation and the plan of redemption. But he did choose to follow God.

We will never in this life be able to tell how many great things went unaccomplished because we lived self-governed lives. Our pride blinds us to see that God has better and more beautiful plans that we can imagine. That same pride wants us to feel our desires for good are greater than our Father's in heaven.

Joshua said to all the people, "This is what the LORD, the God of Israel says: 'From ancient times your fathers lived beyond the Euphrates River, namely, Terah, the father of Abraham and the father of Nahor, and they served other gods. 'Then I took your father Abraham from beyond the

Euphrates River and led him through all the land of Canaan, and multiplied his descendants and gave him Isaac.

Joshua 24:2-3 NASB

Can you be happy and fulfilled following God or do you need to lead?

Have you discovered meaningful ways to leave behind your old gods, your old ways and follow God into the adventure He has for you?

How high on your priority list is being a good follower?

Can you teach your children how to live a joy-filled life of following or do you need to be in control of all the outcomes?

Old and Open

I have already mentioned vision in a negative light. Now I want to unfold vision in a new light. This vision is not from the soul but from the Lord.

Terah was not a young man when he received his call to uproot his life and move on. Terah was not a young man seeking to make his mark in the world; he was not forty. Terah could have been well over a hundred.

He was settled in with three children and most likely everyday life was working out. Even if it wasn't the best life, it was a life he had decades of experience with.

Terah lived seventy years, and fathered Abram, Nahor, and Haran.

As Terah approached one hundred he was going to wrestle with new truth, new light, the challenges for venturing out and leaving what is familiar. In our older age we are usually settling in; Terah is packing to go. Why?

The Bible doesn't tell us.

Terah is living before the covenant, before the law, before his son would establish the faith. We have no clue how things worked. Did God speak in a dream or vision? Did God prompt his heart or simply make him uncomfortable? We don't know.

And in not knowing we have an insight as to how we should live. We should live with the revelation that God has given us.

We should use our Bible and the gift of the Holy Spirit wisely. We should open our hearts to visions and dreams like the earthly father of Jesus – Joseph. We should step back from controlling outcomes and seek to have the Holy Spirit overshadow our lives and direct our steps in any and every way He sees fit.

So if you are an older man, maybe of adult kids, is your time over? Are you past that moment when God can call you to an unseen adventure?

Or if you are a younger father, are you in a hurry? Do you feel like there is some unseen clock counting down the moments until your opportunity is gone?

No father has anything to fear as long as we stay open to the Lord's leading all the days of our lives.

Have you ever found yourself defending a position or an idea because it protects you more than it reflects on the nature of God?

Have you developed the skills of being navigated by God? What does that look like for you? Remember that almost everyone in the Bible was led by God in a distinct and varied way.

Do you have confidence in your relationship with God or do you tend to have more confidence in your systems or methods?

If God leads you to do a new thing in your old age, write it down. Someone coming after you will need to know.

Go

Most of us have little experience with events that do not have an intended outcome.

And honestly, we just don't know how much Terah knew. We don't know if God gave him specific instructions. Maybe he had a lot of details from a dream or vision. Maybe he had none.

Yet as the story of God is told, Terah is a father who packs up and goes.

Now Terah took his son Abram, and Lot the son of Haran, his grandson, and his daughter-in-law Sarai, his son Abram's wife, and they departed together from Ur of the Chaldeans to go to the land of Canaan; and they went as far as Haran and settled there

What do you need in your life to have a "go" or "no go"?

What needs to happen in your life that empowers you to risk your family?

Those are important questions to wrestle with God about. God often helps us grow into knowing. He grows His values in us over time, giving us opportunity to mature. God is our father and like a father He isn't that interested in us just doing the right thing. God is interested in us being the right kind of people. God is interested in a strong, secure relationship.

And truthfully, if you have a healthy relationship with God you can fail some tests. You can miss the mark and get right back on the narrow way because God is fathering you and redeeming you.

As I said earlier, if you are in a covenant relationship with God He is not just interested in using you for His redemptive purpose. His redemptive purpose is to redeem you too.

So, how can you have a relationship with God that is more dependent on love and obedience than circumstances and ideas?

Is there a daily habit you could create that would be training for bigger life lessons?

How much pressure do you place on your life to do things right? Do you live free with a humble heart of obedience? Are you quick to repent but also quick to try?

And most of all, how free are you from comparison? Do you determine how you are doing by comparison, even comparing to Biblical characters?

Or do you have a healthy and whole relationship with your Father in heaven, being open to His promptings, confirmations, and encouragement?

Deep Sorrow

What you are about to read, I in no way take lightly.

There are many sorrows in life and most of them can be taken in stride. But the death of a child is not a sorrow we walk through. We crawl.

And that sorrow is endured by both those who lose the physical life of a child and those who lose the spiritual life of a child. The inability to love and care for those given to us by God can lead to a dark pit of anxiety, guilt, shame, and suffering.

Haran died during the lifetime of his father Terah in the land of his birth, in Ur of the Chaldeans.

Terah had a boy that died.

Let's stop right there for a moment and allow ourselves to feel the pain of that.

Here is a man that is starting the journey of faith for the world. Here is a man whose other son is going to be called the Father of the Faith. He is a man who knows what real life is like. He knows death. He knows sorrow.

Some people say that we cannot be prepared for all the stuff that will happen in life. And for the most part I agree. But I also know we can prepare for all that stuff by not wasting our relationship with our Father in heaven.

I am not saying that if you have a good relationship with God everything will be easy. I am not saying that. I am saying that an authentic relationship with God will help, it will heal, and it will give you a place to rest when there is no safe place on earth.

And Terah's story is like many stories. We don't know why Haran, his son, died. We are left in the dark.

So, Dad, if you are in deep sorrow because of the death of a child I want to give you a big hug and whisper in your ear, keep going. Don't surrender your life to sorrow. Find someone to help you pull that sorrow into the light.

Will you have painful memories all your life – probably. Will you have questions all your life – most likely. So you will need to find what others have discovered. How can I have a relationship with God that sustains me through the deep sorrows of life?

You may first of all need to discover some simple breathing exercises to keep you going. You may need someone to listen without judgment and with empathy. You may need to take time off for retreat and encircle your life with a thousand friends. But at some point, in time you will need God to be your Father. And in His Fathering, you, you will learn to help others through a season of great suffering.

What is my normal cycle of suffering? Do I turn to the Lord quickly and easily or do I tend to carry the burden alone?

Have I hidden feelings and emotions from God and others, or do I trust God with my heart, knowing that He also knows about deep sorrow?

Maybe I have dealt with my sorrow by suppressing it, shoving it down. Can I humbly stand before my Father in heaven with an open heart? Can I trust God to hold me together when I cannot hold myself?

You Are Not Your Child

If we father the way God fathers, we help our children do what they are called to do.

Our children are a part of us. And our children are their own people. Our role is to help them become the people who become the people who raise up other people.

A healthy family helps individuals unite and find both support and service. The basics of life with God are learned in the family setting. In some ways the Great Commission is a call to go and help make God's family.

Things go bad when the parent lives through the child or when the child lives enabling the parent. Life is complicated and few Biblical families made it through life without some grand mistakes.

But mistakes and failures are not the deciding factor. God is.

So regardless of how well you have done so far, lean on the Lord to do better. Don't justify yourself. Don't try to defend your missteps by rehearsing your past, your failed parents, or your social conditions. Breathe in deep the love and grace of God and set your heart to release your child into the future with God.

Your calling, your identity, and your part is to help your children. It is not to be them or even guarantee that they do the "right" thing. You are free to do and be exactly what God has called you to be. You have enough pressure on your life to be fully God's, fully holy, fully obedient. You do not need to try and do all that for yourself and your kids.

So why do we do it?

Are you trying to keep your children from pain and suffering? If so, be honest with God and unfold that fear with Him.

Are you feeling your life is supposed to be an expression of their life? Do you feel your children are yours and as such should live the life you want them to live? Are your children obliged to choose the mate, home, and joy you desire for them? Is that God's idea of Father?

Maybe you are just seeking to help your child be successful. If so, what skills can you impart to them without having a controlling spirit? How can you be more like the Holy Spirit and less like a holy terror?

Barren

Terah was still the head of the family when his son Abram got married. Having multiple generations living in the same household seems a little strange for us but this was normal for Terah and his family.

Being a father also meant being a grandfather and a great-grandfather all in the same house.

When people live together on that level they experience most every part of life together. The events of one person's life are not hidden in a separate room. The hurts or sorrows of the day do not require a phone call or facetime to connect. The joys and sorrows of the family are surrounding you.

So the joy Terah had in being dad also involved the reality that his son would not be a dad.

Sarai was unable to conceive; she did not have a child.

I am sure Terah and Abram shared this sorrow with one another. This family was separated from their previous culture. The journey of living as sojourners was a present reality. And Abram and Sarai faced the reality that children might not be a part of their life together.

As I look at this passage I see one of the greatest challenges any father faces. How do you help your children face the present reality and yet have hope for a wonderful future?

In my sanctified imagination I see Terah using his experience of following some unknown longing and separating his life from his previous life and culture. We simply don't know if Terah's actions were based on spirit, flesh, or circumstances. But as we read God's story, we see that the Lord is orchestrating things for a new family to emerge upon the earth. Even though Terah was still a worshiper of other gods, he was called by Yahweh to take these first steps with his family.

So, for me, that is what fathers need to impart to their children. **God is doing things we cannot see or understand.** Some of those things will only come to light in eternity. Some will be wonderful encounters with God while we are on the earth.

The key to this lesson being passed on is our ability to embrace relinquishment of outcomes and still maintain wholehearted trust in God with an active spirit of asking, seeking, and knocking.

OK, that is a subject of a rather big book. But here I want you to look at the life of Terah and Abram his child and say, "With God the man who will never be a dad can become the father of an entire nation."

As a dad you stand between your child's reality and God. You embrace both the child and God and in the face of their situation you echo the hope of our eternal Father. Not with the intent of producing certain outcomes, but with the overwhelming hope in the nature and character of your Father in heaven.

To our children with limited skills or broken bodies we speak. To our children with disorders or special needs we speak. To our children with fears or emotions or addictions we stand between them and the Lord and echo His hope.

One more thing for dads who have children who have made devastating choices and now face severe consequences. The power of personal choice does not rule the world.

> *The power of personal choice does not rule the world.*

Abram, the child of Terah, has yet to live his life and in that life he will make a lot of bad choices. Some of those choices we look at today and honestly wonder how in the world did God let him get away with that?

But the key to understanding what was going on is that Abram was not "getting away." Abram was living with God. And God was going to both hold Abram accountable and help Abram fulfill his calling on the earth.

And He would start by bringing life from barrenness.

Your greatest pain might be your motivation for your greatest good.

As a dad, how are you at relinquishing outcomes and yet actively hoping, seeking, and praying?

Have you ever pondered how the solution to a problem might be very different from the redemption of a problem? What might that difference mean to your situation or struggle in your life?

Many people face the exact opposite of the promise they feel God has given to them. How is it for our good that we become overcomers in our lives and live in relationship with God regardless of circumstances?

How does the emphasis on relationships protect us and our children from being God's judge and empower us to be God's followers?

Dads Die

Once again, we face the pain and suffering involved with death.

Teaching our children to receive comfort from God, to be aware of eternal life and to be hopeful in the face of suffering is not an American thing. But while we have been focusing on success, Christians all around the world have focused on eternity. And they have raised children of faith in the worst of earthly conditions.

Fathers help their children learn that we do not live to this life alone. And when we do that, a child's identity, their worth and their success is not determined by earthly conditions. **One of the greatest things a dad can do is help their child see that life excels beyond the grave.**

The vision of eternal life does not diminish the importance or significance of this life. It only puts it into perspective. And that perspective takes all the pain and suffering, sorrow and shame and balances it with life eternal in the presence of God.

1 Peter ends with Peter sharing with his readers how they are like a plant, but not a natural plant. He tells them that all the plants of the earth grow and die. But all those who have heard the call of God have responded to the seed.

This seed is the living word of God that does not perish. Then Peter shares this Old Testament truth.

For, "ALL FLESH IS LIKE GRASS, AND ALL ITS GLORY IS LIKE THE FLOWER OF GRASS. THE GRASS WITHERS, AND THE FLOWER FALLS OFF, BUT THE WORD OF THE LORD ENDURES FOREVER." And this is the word which was preached to you.

1 Peter 1:24-25 NASB

When we look at the life of Jesus we see the cross, His death and His transformation. When we look at the life of Peter and his readers we see the cross of suffering in their lives, their death and then their transformation into heaven with God. We see that same thing foreshadowed here.

Your life is the burden you bear. Then you will die. THEN you can enter into life eternal – the Promised Land.

While for Terah and Abram that order is not yet established. They are establishing it. This dad and his child are living out the way that is yet to come.

Are you at peace with the burden of life, the eminence of your death and your transition into eternity?

While we live life here on Earth with God and have hope every day, how can an overemphasis of this life diminish our mental and spiritual health?

How can you prepare your children, in a healthy and whole way, to face the challenges of death? How can you help them have peace when you die? This possibility might rest upon your peace manifested in your life as you trust God and embrace the reality of the bigger life with God yet to come.

Legacy

Hopefully your children will outlive you and they will continue to impact the earth for the glory of the Lord.

When that happens, we often see that some fruit was provided by the parents and passed onto the children. And while it is true that a child can accomplish much without any spiritual heritage, the illustration and importance of family in the Bible is significant.

So once again I am turning to my sanctified imagination and addressing four topics under the heading "Legacy." And it is my personal hope that both you and I can pass on some wisdom to our children in these areas.

- Chosen
- Led
- Promises
- The Promise Land

Joshua said to all the people, "This is what the LORD, the God of Israel says:

*'From ancient times your fathers lived
beyond the Euphrates River, namely,
Terah, the father of Abraham and the
father of Nahor, and they served other
gods. 'Then I took your father Abraham
from beyond the Euphrates River and led
him through all the land of Canaan, and
multiplied his descendants and gave him
Isaac.*

Joshua 24:2-3 NASB

Chosen

When God chooses us we are called to leave the I am that we are and join the "I Am" that He is. His overshadowing presence becomes the thing that gives us an identity, purpose, value, and security. Being chosen by God results in our transformation on the earth into something more like heaven. Not completely like heaven but more like it.

In the past this transformation was known as holiness. Historically transformation has been seen as a transition from the ways of this world to higher ways. Christians have faced mocking about this call to be holy and our failures have been judged by the world as evidence that holiness does not truly exist. But those judgments and mocking do not negate the reality that you are called to be like God, and He is holy.

As a Father you have the burden of helping your child see their life as secure and significant, not through earthly merit or achievement, but through God's divine choice of them.

They are forever loved, not because they are lovely in and of themselves, but because the Lord of all loves them with an everlasting love. Embracing this truth and not making love a condition of performance, will free your child from the guilt and shame of sin and at the same time teach them to live holy because of the unending flow of love for them from the Father.

While striving to be loved can destroy a life, the opportunity to respond to love reveals our personal power to reflect back to others what has been invested into our own lives. In the Biblical sense, the life of God placed in us emerges from us to shine upon others.

And like Abram, a child's pathway might have many significant mistakes. They might discover more failures than successes. But be patient, loving and prayerful. Many of us have children who have great success only after a long road of defeat.

As a Father do you see yourself and your children as having been chosen by God or do you tend to think that you chose God? What is the difference? Think about being picked for a team.

This new team involves a transition away from who you are and into who God desires you to be. What do you think that transition will look like? Will it be fast, slow or both? Will it be a steady progression up or have highs and lows?

How do you judge life now that you are on God's team? Do you determine success by circumstance or wealth? Do you keep a moral scorecard or focus on how personal and intimate your relationship with God is?

If you could do one thing consistently that would help you and your children remember that you have been chosen by God, what would that be?

From the section of scripture quoted earlier there is the phrase, "from the ancient of times." This idea of a long time is hard for modern dads.

In the days of Terah going to town might take a day or two. Getting drinking water might only take an hour or two. What we can do in moments often took them many hours.

So it is quite natural for us to read the Bible and think what we have read in a few moments only took a small amount of time. That would not have been the case. Often what we read in a morning devotion is a story or event that transpired over a decade.

This realization of what transpires over time relates to God's leadership, which does not drive his people. He leads them.

In our world of busy, hurry, rush and panic, the ways of God seem strange. What is urgent for us is often not even essential for a joy-filled life. Our demands for high-speed internet are motivated by a desire to consume content. We are bombarded with false truths that say we are what we accomplish. The meaning and purpose of life can be governed by what we know, what we see, what we encounter in this life. The whole idea of being led in life can be lost in our culture of personal choice and self-rule.

Come with me for a moment to another place. It is a place that fathers have come to often over the centuries. It is a place we discover when life is too difficult or we face discouragement or encounter overwhelming pain. It is the place described in Psalms 23.

A Psalm of David.

The LORD is my shepherd, I will not be in need. He lets me lie down in green pastures; He leads me beside quiet waters. He restores my soul; He guides me in the paths of righteousness for the sake of His name. Even though I walk through the valley of the shadow of death, I fear no evil, for You are with me; Your rod and Your staff, they comfort me. You prepare a table before me in the presence of my enemies; You have anointed my head with oil; My cup overflows. Certainly goodness and faithfulness will follow me all the days of my life, and my dwelling will be in the house of the LORD forever. NASB

Our Father in heaven is a shepherd who leads us. He does not drive us in the modern "driven" sense. Even if you're more familiar with cowboys and cattle drives than sheep and shepherds, you know that the pace of the herd is related to the health of the herd.

Those of us being led by God find all we need because of the nature of God and His leadership style. He leads.

When we fall into the trap of self-living we drive ourselves to produce outcomes and be effective based on production. And while we all desire to be significant because we are worth something, because we can produce, this secondary significance cannot have first place in our lives. We simply do not know all the places we need to go in order to live the life God has for us. Like Tareh, we may need to go to what we do not know so that we can be who God is calling us to be.

The stories of the Bible show us men and women who navigated the life of following God. Some did a great job. Others utterly failed. And yet God unfolds history as a reminder that He is Lord of all and that His people can fully trust Him.

Do you have peace in your life? Do you have time for peace? If not, do you think that is a part of God's plan for your life?

Where do you think the need to be overly busy comes from? Why do we fill our lives with entertainment and recreation? Have you ever had to work so hard at relaxing that you ended up exhausted? How did your last vacation go?

Time is a resource God has given to us all. How God leads us in the use of time will reflect on His care for us and our calling. What we add to our own life reflects our desire for time.

Read Psalms 23 again and then reflect on what follows you. Goodness and faithfulness were the legacy that followed the life of David in this passage. What follows you home from work? What follows you in your family conversation? When you walk into your child's space, what do they see following you?

Promises

We don't know if Terah had any promises from the Lord, but his child did. And as a father you hope that your children have promises from the Lord to live on.

Joshua summarizes the fulfillment of God's promise to Abram and to the people about to enter the Promised Land.

> *Then I took your father Abraham from beyond the Euphrates River and led him through all the land of Canaan, and multiplied his descendants and gave him Isaac.*

Promises are given to help us go somewhere.

This is stated by Peter in his second book. A book written to people struggling on the earth to survive. And just like Abram, they faced trials and tribulations. Peter is writing to people who are involved is several struggles.

> *for His divine power has granted to us everything pertaining to life and godliness, through the true knowledge of Him who called us by His own glory and excellence. Through these He has granted to us His precious and magnificent promises, so that by them you may become partakers of the divine nature, having escaped the corruption that is in the world on account of lust.*
>
> *2 Peter 1:3-4 NASB*

So how do we use promises?

Are promises given to us by God to make life easier or to make us stronger, more enduring, and hopeful?

We all want life to be as easy as possible. There is nothing wrong with that. But an easy life is not the goal. The goal is to glorify God with our life and often that involves hardship and struggles. But there is a context for the struggles.

God gives you a promise so that in the middle of the hardships you face, you can look at His divine nature. I know it is a weird plan, but it works. A promise of God to us, gets embedded in our soul, and when the soul is overwhelmed, the promise of God comes out in the form of His divine nature.

Ok, not always. But that is the plan. That is the way God intends it. And it is OK with Him that it is messy, often imperfect, accomplished in small steps and looks more like a busy kitchen than a finely prepared meal.

Life is lived in the context of the chaos of this world. And just as the Holy Spirit brooded over the chaos at creation, that same Spirit broods over the chaos of your life and seeks to bring creation out of the chaos.

That is why we can slow down, follow, and ponder the promises. Much of what is happening around us is just chaos, noise, and movement. When the Holy Spirit is active we have something more than our own efforts. We can live life leaning on the promises of God. This walking stick helps us to walk in step with the Lord and avoid the frantic pace of life this world seems to seek so often.

Do you have some meaningful scriptures that God has impressed on you repeatedly throughout your life?

Is there a song or a phrase that keeps coming up in your soul during hard or pressing times?

Have people told you the same words or passages of scripture repeatedly?

Some people call these foundational, repetitive scriptures for our lives, life verses. If you feel like you have one or several of these make sure you write them down and ponder them often.

Talk to your children and see if they have a sense of purpose or direction given by God through a verse or phrase. If they do, add that to your prayer list for them.

Finally, make sure your family knows your promises. When your life is over it would be great for them to stand like Joshua of old and say, this is what God promised to do – and He did it.

Promised Land

This is the last of our investigations. It deals with the place God has for us.

It can be easy to make the spiritual life all about thoughts, ideas, mindsets, and unseen things. But the life God calls us to involves our bodies and this physical earth.

So how much space, how big a place do we get here on earth? What does the promise of God look like in my life?

That all depends on His calling and purpose. While we can sing and proclaim that "all the promises of God are ours" we know in our soul that is not true. We see clearly when we read the Bible that not everyone got the same rewards on earth. We see that some carry heavy burdens and others live mostly at peace. The life God gives us is ours and each promise is personalized by the Holy Spirit.

The "one size fits all" style does not work in the clothing world, and it does not work for the promises of God either. And yet, there are plenty of promises that are given to us all, promises that he will never leave or forsake us. Promises of His forgiveness and mercy. These are the universal promises of God, promises for all of us.

But we can fall into the trap of comparison. And many of us not only fall into that trap, but jump in. We have been

48

trained that "what God has done for others he will do for you."

So, we can look at the blessing of others and say, "that is for me." Yet if these blessings are not to be achieved, if we discover that the Promised Land, we claimed is still uninhabited, we are pressured either to double down on the promise or secretly give up.

It is common when comparing to others to feel like your faith is at fault or that God favors someone just a little more than you. Comparison makes us judge ourselves and others, even God, by visible results and not by our callings and purpose. Seldom do we look at the hardships and suffering of faithful Christians and compare ourselves to them. When was the last time you compared your life to someone in the persecuted church or to a martyr?

I'm not trying to be controversial. I'm trying to help you be a father who impacts the life of your children in eternal ways. Some of our kids are going to face difficult times. Some of them are probably in difficult times right now.

God has a place for them. They have a place to belong. Their eternal home is the most significant. The reality of life with God in heaven is of first importance.

They also have a land of promise here. But the here and now land may be filled with giants, trials, pain, and suffering. Each person's unique calling results in conditions and results that cannot be recognized by comparing. What might be a radical success for one is obtained by not even trying for another.

We need to help our children see that faithfulness to God regardless of how hard, easy, or externally rewarding it maybe, IS the way. **Obedience verifies love for God.** Obedience will make a place for you on earth, but it will also decide what that place looks like.

The gifts and grace of God establish the land of promise God has for you, regardless of its condition. And often the work of God on earth is multigenerational. We start something, another completes. Or maybe we complete what others have started. The success of life in Christ Jesus is never ours alone. We are helped and help others all along the way.

Because life is multigenerational and because you are raising the next generation, make your home a haven. To the best of your ability, be a dad who makes home a land of promise. A place to belong. A place to make mistakes and learn. A place that quickly forgives and yet speaks the truth in love, avoiding the sins of sweeping things under the rug.

Be a dad who provides a place, a sacred place, as you lead in a shepherd's style.

How much do I care about my home? Is it just a place to eat and sleep or is it more?

What practical things need to be addressed so that we can have more space for belonging? What stuff do we care too much about that might need to be reduced or provide freedom from care and maintaining?

Am I living more by comparison than by sonship? Do I trust God's plan for me, or do I keep needing confirmation in contrast to others?

How is my energy level when it comes to establishing my home as a promised land? Do I have fears? Have I experienced rejection or hostility in the past when I have tried to move in this direction?

Now Terah took his son Abram, and Lot the son of Haran, his grandson, and his daughter-in-law Sarai, his son Abram's wife, and they departed together from Ur of the Chaldeans to go to the land of Canaan; and they went as far as Haran and settled there.

Terah didn't make it to the promised land.

Many of us have been raised under the mindset that if we are not everything, we are nothing. Maybe you have heard a sermon or two on this passage about how Terah was a failure, he made it only halfway.

I don't believe that.

The story of dads on the earth is that we each carry the burden a few steps. We advance the Kingdom of God; we don't fulfill it. And that is OK.

There is one who holds all things together, one who is the Alpha and Omega, one who is the Eternal Wise and All Knowing, and we are not Him. I'm OK with that.

But as a Father I long to love God and my kids. I long to do my part in this journey with the Lord. I am sure you do too.

So, I hope this little book helps you. I know in writing it, it has helped me. It has helped me gain perspective and a little wisdom. To see that while my heart often desires to be Abraham, I am more like his dad. My life is more hidden, more a movement than fulfillment, more a transition out of darkness than an unfolding of the light.

And it has helped me be content. A contentment that allows me to enjoy the life I have more and reject the pressure to obtain a promise and a calling reserved for another, maybe my children.

Thanks Dad for reading this and I pray that you and your Father in heaven continually enjoy your journey together.

Scriptures on Terah

In just over two hundred and fifty English words we have the life of a father recorded for us. Many fathers have had fewer words. Most of the men who have lived have no Biblical record at all.

Just as we do not know all the fathers who have gone before us we also do not know all the fathers who are living today. Great men and evil men are here together. We know a few. We read books about some of the most popular, those who have obtained accomplishments or notoriety. But most fathers we simply do not know about.

As you read through these words about Terah, open your heart to hear from God.

What is our Father in heaven revealing about faithfulness, or transition?

What does God want us to understand about generations and time?

What can we see here that might help us live with full hearts as we sojourn here on earth?

Biblical Passages

And Serug lived two hundred years after he fathered Nahor, and he fathered other sons and daughters. Nahor lived twenty-nine years, and fathered Terah; and Nahor lived 119 years after he fathered Terah, and he fathered other sons and daughters. Terah lived seventy years, and fathered Abram, Nahor, and Haran.

Now these are the records of the generations of Terah. Terah fathered Abram, Nahor, and Haran; and Haran fathered Lot. Haran died during the lifetime of his father Terah in the land of his birth, in Ur of the Chaldeans. Abram and Nahor took wives for themselves. The name of Abram's wife was Sarai, and the name of Nahor's wife was Milcah, the daughter of Haran, the father of Milcah and Iscah. Sarai was unable to conceive; she did not have a child.

Now Terah took his son Abram, and Lot the son of Haran, his grandson, and his daughter-in-law Sarai, his son Abram's wife, and they departed together from Ur of the Chaldeans to go to the land of Canaan; and they went as far as Haran and settled there. The days of Terah were 205 years; and Terah died in Haran.

Genesis 11:23-32 NASB

Joshua said to all the people, "This is what the LORD, the God of Israel says: 'From ancient times your fathers lived beyond the Euphrates River, namely, Terah, the father of Abraham and the father of Nahor, and they served other gods. 'Then I took your father Abraham from beyond the Euphrates River and led him through all the land of Canaan, and multiplied his descendants and gave him Isaac.

Joshua 24:2-3 NASB

Serug, Nahor, Terah, and Abram, that is Abraham.

1 Chronicles 1:26-27 NASB

the son of Amminadab, the son of Admin, the son of Ram, the son of Hezron, the son of Perez, the son of Judah, the son of Jacob, the son of Isaac, the son of Abraham, the son of Terah, the son of Nahor,

Luke 3:33-34 NASB